The Nature Kid's Guide to
ORCAS

DAVID ANDERSON

LP Media Inc. Publishing
Text copyright © 2026 by LP Media Inc.
All rights reserved.

For information address LP Media Inc. Publishing,
30012 Variolite St NW, Princeton MN 55371
www.lpmedia.org

Publication Data

Orcas
The Nature Kid's Guide to Orcas — First edition.

Summary: "Learn all about Orcas, the Nature Kid Way"
— Provided by publisher.

ISBN: 979-8-89818-132-1

[1. Orcas – Non-Fiction] I. Title.

Title: The Nature Kid's Guide to Orcas

CONTENTS

COLD COASTS

An orca can hold its breath for up to 15 minutes and dive 500 feet deep!

Splash! A huge orca bursts from the cold, dark sea.

Orcas live in cool ocean waters. They swim near rocky coasts and icy shores where the sea runs deep and full of life.

These bold animals are easy to spot. Their black and white skin stands out against the blue waves. You can see them pop up near cliffs, bays, and islands.

Cold coasts give orcas everything they need. Waves bring lots of food close to shore. It is the perfect place to call home.

OCEAN ORBITS

Some orcas near Antarctica swim 5,000 miles to warm water and back each year!

Whoosh! An orca pod races through the wide open ocean.

Orcas swim in every ocean on Earth. Cold water near the poles is where they thrive — that is where food is most plentiful and where the biggest populations live.

Some orcas do venture into warmer tropical waters, but not to stay. Scientists have discovered they make these long trips to shed old skin in the warmer water, then race back to the cold.

One **pod** may swim 100 miles in a single day. No other large ocean hunter covers as much ground. Orcas are true ocean explorers.

MEGA MAMMALS

A male orca weighs as much as three hippos put together!

Boom! A giant orca crashes down into the sea with a splash.

Orcas are the biggest dolphins on Earth. A male can grow up to 30 feet long. That is as long as a school bus!

Males weigh up to 12,000 pounds. That is heavier than a big truck! Females are smaller but still very strong and fast.

Next to a person, an orca is huge. You would only reach its belly! These mighty animals are some of the biggest hunters in the sea.

BUILT BOLD

DID YOU KNOW?
Every orca has a unique gray mark near its fin, just like a fingerprint!

Swoosh! A tall black fin cuts through the waves like a sail.

Orcas have smooth, strong bodies built for the sea. A thick layer of fat called **blubber** keeps them warm in icy water. Their slick skin helps them glide without slowing down.

A tall fin sits on top of an orca's back. It is called a **dorsal fin**. On a male, this fin can stand 6 feet tall! Flippers on each side help the orca steer and turn.

Orcas breathe through a hole on top of their head called a **blowhole**. They must come up to the surface for each breath of air.

CLICK, CLICK

Each orca family has its own special calls, like a secret language only they understand!

Click, click, click! An orca sends sounds into the dark sea.

Orcas use sound to find their way. They make clicks that bounce off things nearby. This is called **echolocation**.

Those clicks come back like echoes. They tell the orca what is around it. An orca can find a single fish in dark, murky water from far away!

Orcas also see very well both above and below the waves. Their sharp senses make them expert hunters in any conditions.

TOP TOUGH

Crack! An orca snaps its jaws with power and might.

Orcas are built to be tough. Their strong jaws and big bodies scare other animals away. No creature in the sea wants to fight one.

An orca has about 50 sharp teeth. Each one is curved to grab and hold slippery prey. Their bite is one of the strongest in the ocean.

All of this makes orcas very hard to beat. Their body is like a weapon. They are the toughest animals in the sea, and they know it.

Orca teeth can be 4 inches long and never fall out or grow back!

FISHY FEASTS

Gulp! An orca swallows a big salmon in one giant bite.

Orcas eat many kinds of sea animals. Some groups eat only fish. Others hunt seals, squid, and even whales much bigger than themselves.

Some orcas love salmon best. They prefer big, fatty fish full of energy. Each orca can eat 300 to 500 pounds of food a day!

Other orcas hunt bigger animals like sea lions or stingrays. What they eat depends on where they live and what their family taught them.

Some orcas hunt great white sharks and eat only their livers!

TEAM TRAP

Orcas create waves on purpose to knock seals right off floating ice!

Slap! The orcas smack their tails and push fish together.

Orcas hunt as a team. They talk with clicks and calls to make a plan. Then they work together to catch food.

Some orcas herd fish into a tight ball near the surface. Then they take turns swimming through it. Each one grabs a mouthful of fish!

Other orcas circle seals near the shore. They take turns chasing until the seal gets tired. Working together helps them catch even the fastest prey.

NO FOES

Whomp! The orca charges, and every sea creature swims away.

Orcas sit at the very top of the food chain. No animal in the ocean hunts them. They are the top hunter of the sea.

Even big sharks stay away from orcas. A great white may be tough, but an orca is tougher. Orcas are bigger, faster, and much smarter.

Being at the top means orcas have no predators. Nothing tries to eat them. They truly rule the ocean.

When orcas show up, great white sharks flee and stay away for months!

STAY SAFE

Swish! The orca pod moves close and swims as one big group.

Orcas stay safe by sticking together. A pod swims as a group and looks out for each other at all times.

When a young orca needs help, adults rush over. They swim around it in a tight circle. This keeps the calf safe from any harm.

The ocean can be a wild place. But a pod keeps every orca safe. There is always safety in numbers, and orcas never swim alone.

Orcas have been seen pushing a sick family member to the surface to breathe!

WATER ROCKETS

At full speed, an orca swims 34 miles per hour—faster than most boats!

Zoom! An orca shoots through the water like a torpedo.

Orcas are fast and powerful swimmers. They pump their strong tails up and down. This pushes them through the water at amazing speeds.

Orcas can zip along for hours without rest. They swim all day to find food. A pod may cover 75 miles or more in a single morning.

Orcas also love to leap from the water. This is called breaching. They twist in the air and crash back with a giant splash!

BUSY
BODIES

Thwap! An orca smacks the water with its flipper at dawn.

Orcas are busy all day long. They spend the morning looking for food. Then they rest and play in the afternoon.

Orcas love to play! They chase each other and surf on waves. Young orcas toss seaweed with their fins just for fun.

At night, orcas slow down to rest. They float near the surface and barely move. But even then, they never completely fall asleep.

Orcas sleep with one eye open, resting only half their brain at a time!

POD PALS

FUN FACT!
Some orca pods have over 40 members spanning four generations!

Squeal! A young orca calls out to its family swimming nearby.

Orcas live in groups called pods. A pod is like a big family. They eat, travel, and play together every single day.

The oldest female leads the pod. She knows where to find food and shows the younger orcas the best spots. Everyone follows her.

Pod members stay together for life. They share food and care for each other through good times and bad. The bond between orcas is one of the strongest in nature.

LOVE CALLS

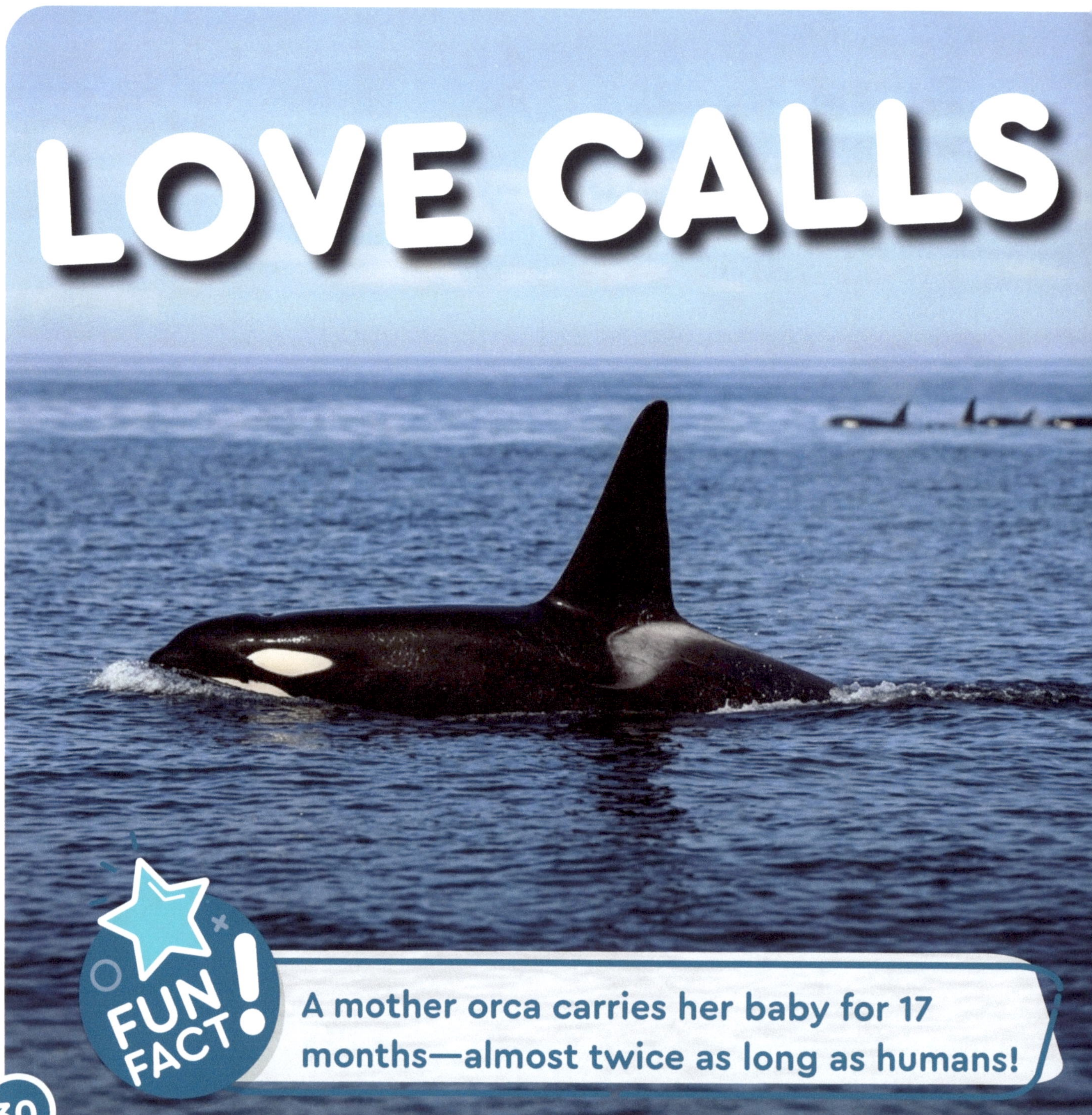

FUN FACT!
A mother orca carries her baby for 17 months—almost twice as long as humans!

Squeak! A male orca swims to a new pod to find a mate.

Orcas do not mate in their own pod. Males swim to other groups to find a mate. This keeps orca families strong and healthy.

Males show off to get noticed. They may leap high or slap the water hard. A healthy male with a tall fin has the best chance.

After mating, the male goes home to his own pod. The female stays with her family. She will carry the baby for a very long time before it is born.

CUTE
CALVES

Plop! A brand new orca calf drops into the cold sea.

Orca calves are born in the water. The mother helps the baby swim to the surface right away. It takes its first breath of air within seconds.

A newborn calf weighs about 400 pounds. It is around 7 feet long. Even as a baby, an orca is bigger than most grown-up dolphins!

The calf stays close to its mother at all times. It drinks rich milk to grow fast. In just one year, it can double in size!

Baby orcas are born with orange patches that slowly turn white as they grow!

MOM MATTERS

Grandma orcas help the whole pod survive—pods with grandmas catch more fish!

Bump! A mother orca pushes her little calf through the waves.

Orca mothers take great care of their young. They teach calves how to hunt and find food. The calf learns by watching and copying every move.

A mother shares her food with her calf. She breaks fish into small pieces so the calf can eat. This goes on until it can hunt alone.

Orca mothers stay close to their young for many years. Some sons never leave their mother's side, even as adults. It is one of the strongest bonds in all of nature.

DIRTY WATERS

Blub! An orca swims slowly through dark and dirty water.

Orcas face many dangers from people. Dirty water and poison flow into the sea. This can make orcas very sick over time.

Ships and boats make the ocean loud. That noise can hurt the way orcas hear and talk to each other. It makes finding food much harder.

Some orcas run low on food, too. The fish they need are harder to find each year. When fish go away, orcas go hungry.

Pollution can pass from mother orcas to their calves through milk!

HELP OUT

FUN
FACT!
Only about 75 Southern Resident orcas remain—but their numbers are slowly rising!

Hooray! An orca leaps as people cheer from the shore.

People are working hard to save orcas. They are cleaning up the oceans and making new rules. Laws now stop boats from getting too close to pods.

Groups are fixing rivers so salmon can return. More fish means more food for hungry orcas. This important work helps orca families grow stronger.

You can help orcas, too! Keep beaches clean and use less plastic. Every small act helps keep the ocean safe for these amazing animals.

GLOSSARY

pod
A group of orcas that live and travel together like a family

blubber
A thick layer of fat under the skin that keeps an orca warm

blowhole
A hole on top of an orca's head used for breathing

dorsal fin
The tall fin on top of an orca's back

echolocation
Using sound clicks that bounce back to find things in water